CW01649850

Weightless Pedestrian

Gareth Strachan

For :

Everyone who has ever said 'hello' to me,
particularly the first ones :
Ma and Da.

Group Hug Includes :

Guddha

Aunty Sue & Sheila

Sister Larry Brother James

Jackie Wills BBC Thomson

Festival Glen Festival Pam

Maddy Steggy

Henry Postie Coffee Mark

Manisha Big Mike

J.J.

Proper Canadian Bear Hug extended to the Mustard Collective

Original Drypoint (Cover) & Gnostic Guidance : John T Freeman
Design & Friendship : Malcolm Leyland
Printing & Patience : Repropoint

Everybody needs a neighbour named Nigel…thanks Nigel.

I

Fear of ~~Poverty~~

Fear of Poetry.

I'll write this poem but on one condition…

…The Human Condition.

Far Bee

(Roses are red coz they bled)

Verse is a perverse curse
that I keep coming
back to…

Far be it
from me
to write
prose…

Far better
for me
to water the rose
that gave life to the verse
in the first place.

Last to Leave London

For Raf, Mai & Sako

Always the last
to leave
London.

Left my
train set
there
once.

Left my
left cheek
and my right
mind.

Left my
tube map
in the lap
of an anthill.

Left the
river once.
Then twice.
Then buried
it beneath
a bridge.

Always the last
to leave
London.

They keep moving
the river and the city
won't stay still.

They keep moving
the ice-bergs

and the buildings
won't stay still.

Left my best book
and my best foot
forward.

Left my ego.
Left my underpants.
Left my ego
in my underpants.

Left my new paper.
Left my old paper.
Left my S.U.V.
parked in a disabled space.

Left Wimbledon where it was
and Waterloo in the
middle of a mud base.

Keep leaving London.
Keep leaving stuff
all over London.
Keep going back to
look for it all.
Keep missing the final train home.

(Deep Breath)

They keep moving the
graffiti and the
words won't stay still

Bukowski's Brain*

Beer, boobies, poem, beer, boobies, poem, beer, boobies, poems
Beer, boobies, poem, beer, boobies, poem, beer, boobies, poems
Beer, boobies, poem, beer, boobies, poem, beer, boobies, poems
Beer, boobies, poem, beer, boobies, poem, beer, boobies, poems
Beer, boobies, poem, beer, boobies, poem, beer, boobies, poems
Beer, boobies, poem, beer, boobies, poem, beer, boobies, poems
Beer, boobies, poem, beer, boobies, poem, beer, boobies, poems
Beer, boobies, poem, beer, boobies, poem, beer, boobies, poems
Beer, boobies, poem, beer, boobies, poem, beer, boobies, poems
Beer, boobies, poem, beer, boobies, poem, beer, boobies, poems
Beer, boobies, poem, beer, boobies, poem, beer, boobies, poems
Beer, boobies, poem, beer, boobies, poem, beer, boobies, poems
Beer, boobies, poem, beer, boobies, poem, beer, boobies, poems
Beer, boobies, poem, beer, boobies, poem, beer, boobies, poems
Beer, boobies, poem, beer, boobies, poem, beer, boobies, poems

* For those who are not familiar with the poet Charles Bukowski, this is by far the best introduction, the most accurate biography.

Half-past Love

When he asked her the time
She slipped off her dress
And the big hand
Went over the little one

Virgin Snow, Shivering Sun

Iamma born-again snowflake
Iamma shivering sun
Iamma virgin nightfall
Iamma night fulla' fun

Iamma lotta cold fox fur
Iamma fidgeting mink
Iamma lotta damn long coats
Iamma face fulla' pink

Iamma slippery snowflake
Iamma born-again virgin
Iamma chattering night-watch
I am a shivering man

Haiku 1

between poems
we take
breaths

Future has-been

Art without heart is like soul without flesh – unbearable

Poor Britney

Going nuts is bad enough; doing it in front of the world must be highly distressing

Going Nowhere

I refuse to take the training wheels off this poem until I can fully ride

Cheap One-liners

Can be made better by
two

You Know Are in Love When

You can happily fart in each others' pajamas

The Eyelash

It came in a blank white envelope addressed to 'The Owner': a single, solitary eyelash

Said One Chav to Another

You can take a gift horse to water but you should never look it in the mouth…

Said the Other Chav in Response

…So which one should we bet on…?

The Artist Turns to Blob

She at her paintbrush, all waxy and gaunt; he at his sketchbook, melting by lamplight

The Secret

A Novel takes 300 pages to make its point. Poetry does it in half a page…

The Evolution of Poetry

No better than the burping frog who muzzled his way into existence.
No better than the moaning mud-skipper who crawled out of the water.
No better than the tragic ant carrying the world on her shoulders.
No better than the solitary bear sticking his fingers up at passing traffic.
No better than the persistent raccoons living under the house, rifling through the rubbish, looking for a sugary end to city life.
No better than the last defiant grouse whose fame and fortune are written into chocolate wrappers.
No better than the cursing amoebae sneezing then farting then sneezing then dying.
No better than those slow moving turtles on Galapagos, chewing on Darwin's private papers.
No better than the look of fear in their eyes, with every hungry human that set foot on the island, starving and desperate for anything that tastes like chicken.

No better than
the burping frog's legs.

Haiku 2

scratching at pink head

craning over page

fixing his haiku

Nothing Haunts Me Anymore

Nothing haunts me.
The thought of it.
No ghosts visit me.
I've asked them to,
left out white sheets
for them to hide under.
I've called to them
but it's like
talking to thin air.

And it's this thin
air I want to
be part of…
to float around in,
to be a ghost,
to haunt others,
to say 'boo' with as
much belly as I can muster.

To make the best
of nothing.

<Curious Face Here>

P.T.O.

P.T.O.

P.oetic T.houghts O.mitted

Where Do I Go When the Lights Grow Dim

After Vic Goddard & Subway Sect.

Deep pockets.
Shallow Grave.

Bury us with every
word written under
the sun

that we
might still mutter
in our sleep.

Eye that Shoreline

Eye that shoreline
Eye that wave
Eye that wave hitting that shoreline
Eye that redundant sea air
we go gasping towards

Eye that rat
Eye that red rat
Eye that red rat with the pink lungs
Eye that red rat that wears wigs
and dreams of being on stage

I that shoreline.
I that rat.

The Chimney Pigs

(early december, oh five)

The Chimney Pigs in Fulham
are snorting at the window:

The Chip Shop digs
Where my old pals live
With the rooftop Hogs

The Chimney Pigs
are settling in for the night:

I keep getting drunk.
Putting my brain in the mincer.
Turning the handle slowly.

The Chimney Pigs
woke me up again:

Snorting and grunting.
Farting and sniffing.
Hunting for morning.

The Chimney Pigs
are scoffing at the London sun:

They are grinding to a halt.
They are friendly to a fault.
They are planning a revolt.

When I open the window
they grease up all the walls:

Eat all my books.
Drink all the Pims.
Crap on my floor.

But with the window open
I can breathe more deeply:

I count to sixty.
Wait for them to run.
Find them shivering behind sofas.

Off they trot, the entire lot,
breaking plates & trampling furniture.

They're not in the lardar.
They're not in the toilet.
They're not in the flume.

The Wild Tranquil is in my heart
but The Chimney Pigs are in my room:

They're in my bed.
They're in my head.
They're in the bloody garden shed.

The Chimney Pigs
are grinning at the London Moon.

They got me pinned against the floor.
Drinking my Pims.
Sniffing my armpits for a purpose.

The Chimney Pigs have had they're say.
The Chimney Pigs have told me how it is.

Will not wrestle them.
Will not play tug-of-war with them.
Will roll around in crap with them

And feed them chips.
And snort along.

Three Lions (swallow with water)

Sometimes I think
England's being held
up by matchsticks,
sometimes by my own sinking eyelids
sometimes by solid foundations
sometimes by a crucifx
sometimes my own patience

A Nation of Farmers
A Nation of Moaners

Sometimes I think
I'm being held
up by England,
sometimes by the scruff
sometimes by the collar
sometimes by the late trains
sometimes by the scholar

A Nation of Gardeners
A Nation of Loners

Sometimes I think
we're holding each
other up
sometimes by the rough seas
sometimes by the rolling hills
sometimes by the boundless plains
sometimes by two chalky pills

A Nation of Pardoners
A Nation of Throners

And the Name of This Poem Is…

a series of dots
a series of dots
a series of dots
a series of dots
a series of dots
a series of dots
a series of dots
a series of dots
a series of dots
a series of dots
....

And the Name of This Poem Is

a pile of words
a pile of words
a pile of words
a pile of words
a pile of words
a pile of words
a pile of words
a pile of words
a pile of words
a pile of words
a
pile
ofwords

When the Indians Saw the First Ships

For Elisabetta & Paul

Think of a colour

that does

not exist.

Hold it in your mind.

Hold it tight.

Now –

describe it to me.

Haiku 3

lost her best poem

somewhere between here

and the river

Sunlight

Makes me

sneeze

all over the page.

Once upon a

time

there was the

end.

Midnight Religion

A Church and a Mosque
Got up in the Night
They looked at each other
And started to Fight

Along came a Temple
A Synagogue Too
They shook hands and made plans
To visit the Zoo

After the lions
And tigers and Bears
It was crumpets and trumpets
But no nasty Glares

They talked and they talked,
Looked back on the Ages
'To Bed', they said
And crawled back in their Cages

MIND THE GAP

We would like to take
this opportunity
to publicly declare
that all of our clothing
is made by hand-picked
ORGANIC CHILDREN ONLY!

All of our underage slaves
are **GRAIN-FED & FREE-RANGE!**
Each one is given the
entire length
of the sweat-shop
to roam freely

<Cynical Face Here>

Love Ya

Even in the white death
of a Canadian Wintah:

Even in that yellow
cloud over Chiner:

Even in the thickest
porridge of an English Mornin:

Even under the shade
of the Bodhi Tree:

Even in Mok Dong
Detention Centre:

Love Ya. Miss Ya.

Self Help for the Selfish

(To a Drowning Fraud)

I kick the blanket
off me.
I wriggle free of it

I throw it.
I throw it.

I kick the poet
from my bed.
I kick the poet
like a bucket

A poet.
A poet.

Must be
the Great Fraud
within me.

Must be.
Must be.

I leave the
showmanship
to the arseholes

and the
penmanship

to the past souls

and steer
my own ship
towards my own goals

I tow it.
I tow it.

I kick the blanket
off me.
I wriggle free from it.
I shuck it.
In a sinking ship
I am a bucket.

I throw it.
I throw it.

Throw it overboard
to a drowning Fraud.

< In a sinking ship
I am a bucket >

Fear of ~~Poverty~~

Fear of Poetry.

As a poet, you can be certain of poverty

As a peasant, you cannot be certain of poetry

As a certainty, you can be fearful of both

For either way, you are a broke(n) man

<Brave Face Here>

Cost Benefit Analysis of the Average Modern Poem

Costs	Benefits
Unemployment	Incapacity Benefit
Vanity Publishing	Creative Control
Unfashionable	Post - Modern
Self Obsession	Self Awareness
Delusion	Enlightenment
Crazy Chicks / No Chicks (Both)	Art Chicks / Smart Chicks (Both)

Flatpack Poetry

You manufacture it,
I flatpack it.
You puncture it,
I munch on it.
You punctuate the planet,
I gravitate towards it
and you reward me with granite.

You manufacture souls,
I flatpack them.
You fracture holes in space,
I repair them with grace.
You deviate men,
I alleviate them
and you reward us with opinions.

You fatten the land,
I flatten it.
You flatter it,
I matter-of-fact it.
You point-of-view the earth,
I point towards self-worth
and you reward me with stones.

All Creatures Great & Small

Morning Fruit Fly
Flying by
Wipe the Cobweb
From your Eye
Alive by Five
and then you Die.

Mug of Miracles

You're as mad as a box of frogs.
You're as ugly as a bag of hammers.
You're as painful as bed of nails.
You're as meaningless as a mug of miracles.

By my word, I love you.

Life's a Drag

He can't escape
the perfume scent
when he climbs
into her Sunday Best.

But he really only
feels complete
- only knows its real -

when he's tied on
every tricky pleat,
tried on every heel.

Life's a drag, she whispered…
and then you marry one.

In the Redundant, the Abundant

Eve fell asleep
in Adam's lap today.
He picked the dust
out of her eyes,
pulled the hair out
out of her mouth.
The infinite, she said
in half-moans.
So very small & subtle –
So infinitely small...

In the Redundant,
the Abundant.

Adam squeezes his tea-bag
against the inside of
Eve's cup and
looks miraculous.
Isn't solar power
wonderful, he thinks
noticing how absorbing
she becomes when
the sun hits her face...

In the Redundant
the Abundant.

Oh, to be the Last Twitching Muscle in Stephen Hawking's Mouth

First the earth.
Then the moon.
Then the sun.
Then the rest of
the planets.
Then gravity and
all that goes with it.
All of it and all of us
descending into this
terrific, tiny black dot
at the centre of the universe….

….only to be spat out,
ejaculated, sprayed like
pesticide, back into space,
back onto a blank canvas,
like a messy Jackson Pollock.

The Joy of Verse

Multiverse – Many universes
Miniverse – Apple-sized universe
Introverse – 2nd universe at the end of space
Omniverse – Here & Now

It's all poetry.

What the Richest Creature in the World Says *1

Nothing sedates rationality like large doses of effortless money.

What the Poorest One Says *2

No one buys organic on the dole.

What the Smartest Creature Says *3

It is a serious event to bring a new human being into the world if you can't look after it properly. I was just not ready.

Talking in My Sleep

O Cliché! O Cliché! Perched on my lip - Am I forever in your merciless grip?

Loneliness

Poor old English pub. No one inside. Dog chews carpet. Stares across the road at a line of legs waiting to enter....another damn Yates

And Truth

And truth came upon him like a lizard in Morocco

Sainburys Fields Forever

In aisle seven I bought heaven

Crawling Behind a Snowplough in Sorrow

My eyes are as salty as the roads

Dear Reader

We are nothing without your thoughts on this poem, your thumbs on this page.

* All taken from The Observer 9.3.08
1. Warren Buffet
2. Nick Cohen
3. Marion

Communism

I get smug and jealous
when I read about
the success of other
writers.

I really can't handle it.

I'm only suggesting
we burn
a few books
– *not for their ideology* –
but to remove
the competition.

<this book is fire-proof>

Waiting for Becket (to arrive)

Isn't it enough
to just hold the pen?
Dip the tip
in sugar
and keep the thought

under your tongue.

Serotonin

When will it run out?
When will it run free?
When will it be on the shelves
at every pharmacy?

Goodbye Windy Heathrow

O, to be the
irony
of a slow turning
mill,
on a slow moving
hill
that has only enough
wind
to generate itself.

O, to ask the
wind:
What is
me?
What is the point of
me?
O, to hear the
answer
back in silence.

All Work and No Play (makes Jack a dull boy)

A poem is never finished, only abandoned. A poem is never finished, only aban…
…and so say all of us. (thanks Paul Valery).

II

God Only Nose.

And if darkness wraps
its shawl around me…
…shall wear it proudly
wear it proudly

Losing Faith

Son of a useless God
Son of a meaningless man,
Son of an invisible sod
Son of a godless plan

I'm done with it all.
I'm gonna start a city and name it after my best friend.
I'm gonna call my city *Hank.*

All shall bow down to Hank.
All shall build statues of Him.

I'm gonna write greeting cards,
humourless and sour,
meaningless and dour
in his name.
Hank – what fun…
but I'm done.

I'm done with this sun,
with this transparent pun

with this son –
"*the anointed one*"
of a pointless, sodless,
godless none.

Beautiful Loser

Must be the trusty
loch-keeper
who said it
best:

Keep your river
at your breast.

Optimism

Glass half-full

Pessimism

Glass half-empty

Indifference

Glass half-assed

The Language Demons

And so it is written.
They came by Dawn.
The whole thing was over in minutes.
First they took the word 'Penis'
and shoved it in Happiness.
Next, they summoned the whole of 'Hell'
and hid it in Health.
Then they came for 'Me'
and I was stuffed, kicking and screaming,
into the word 'Meek'.
Lastly, they took 'You'
and holed you up Unanimous, Ubiquitous, Eureka!

And they did it all in the
name of Crown and Country.

We know who they own.
We know who they count.

The whole thing was over in minutes.
And so it is written.

7 Gods

We asked seven of the most
popular Gods to come together
in a room for some light
discussion. We gave them some
triangle sandwiches and some
cans of coke (and straws for the
ones who had trouble sipping
wine out of a can).

We wanted to find out which
one was real, which one was
the genuine article.

Only six showed up and the
seventh, a man the agency
didn't have a picture of, sent
me an apology saying,
*"it's not me but if you ever
want to talk...don't hesitate
to contact my team."*

He left me six useful
contacts and a nice picture
of them all at an office lunch:
smiling, eating triangle sandwiches
and sipping cans of coke
through a straw.

Undressing Each Other with Eyeballs

          To my right,
                    just a little to my right
is a good looking
couple.

And to my left,
just a bit
to the
left

is an ugly looking bloke
with one eye   going   this-a-way
and
          another
going
that-a-way.

Gone are his girlfriends' teeth.
Gone are her eyebrows.
Gone is her hair in the eloquent air.
Gone. Gone with the wind.

You know, the pretty-hot lot
keep looking at the not-hot-lot,
to see if they are looking
at them or at me or at the newspaper…

…and all of our eyes

          do

this   that

          and

the   other…

Ty(p)ing Hands Behind Back

At London Bridge,
there's a project
called 'Open Shutters Iraq'.
Testimonials and horror
stories of how purple blood
stains white sand.
I'm almost brought
to tears but the
Englishmen in me
holds together and
crunches his teeth.

The tourists are
not fazed.
They take pictures
and admire the Thames.

All art is pointless.
All I can do is
write drivel with
hands tied behind backs,
All I can offer is grit:

The astonishing triumph
of the Japanese camera.
The unrivalled smiles
of the children of South London.
The law of life and
the cadence of laughter.

It's all we can offer.
It's the best we can do.
I hope the sand rakes
over the blood in my eyes.

A Harlot in Heaven

Every now and
then she wakes
in a sweat

Brought to sudden
consciousness

By the sheer
awareness

Of her own
subtle heaven

Bumping Heads on Beauty

Lowered guard on God
Brushed an arm on Buddha
Tied the two together
Gave the rope to Guddha

Traced her lines of patience
Danced into a dud
Minced her words in wisdom
Made a claim in mud

Poured himself in hatred
Clambered out of climax
Bored himself with borders
Washed away a waxwork

Spanned a simple lifetime
Bruised her breast on man
Wrung herself in red wine
Tickled pink her plans

Crushed a can of nightmares
Choked a thousand cigs
Parted ways with poets
Watered waves in wigs

Marooned herself in marriage
Caroused herself with children
Amused herself with Armitage
Bemused it all with Bourbon

Concealed their weapons of war
Drunk the Daily News
Knit himself to herself
Entrenched themselves in truths

Bumped their heads on beauty
Bruised their words on bards
Broke their backs on paper
Bound it all in card

Back to Verse 1

Wingspan of Desire

Is truly immeasurable,
my friends.

Take flight.

Haiku 4

water your thinking
watch it grow in tiny ways
place under a red sun

Blake's Tree Spirits

Show themselves
to you

in the boredom
of oblivion.

Two Broken Halves

To a Woman in Distress from a Man in Much the Same

two broken halves
like two crossing paths
meeting in the middle
seeking only simple
things in little glass jars:
planets, people, roads, cars-

closing the lid on it all
closing the lid
on each other
closing the casket on caution
lifting the lid on a lover

oh the cracking sun
oh the vast eternal
oh the broken vase
of the nervous universal

Two Broken Angles < >

Two broken angels
Like two broken angles
Leaning close together
Like two broken anvils
But buckling in the middle
Like two broken ankles

27 Buttercups Burning

The poet would
sooner you
threw the book
on the fire
to keep yourself
warm
than hold it
under his chin
to see if the
words
glow

Look at What the Future Drops

He doesn't know what it holds,
but he knows
it involves a shed
and a small clock.
He knows it involves
the kind of clock
that says, *you really should get up now.*

I cannot believe the sky sometimes.

He knows it involves you,
reaching out for that clock,
calling out for earl grey
at six eh em.
He knows it involves
a woman of such
unrivaled bone structure
that it hurts his jaw
to smile at her.

I cannot believe the sky sometimes.

He knows it involves you
bringing sandwiches
out to the shed,
saying,
for all the clever thoughts you think,
for all the trees you carve
your name in,

for all the time, and despite
the weather,
you never bring the plates back in.

I cannot believe the sky sometimes.

He knows it involves you
dragging a sleeping bag
out to him,
making a pillow amongst
the plates and saucers,
amongst the sacred bits of junk
he refuses to part with.

I cannot believe the sky.

He knows it involves
a view of the moon
and only enough room
in the shed
for two heads
on one pillow
and two sets of feet
pointing to other planets.

There is no sky.

He knows it involves
the drop of night
like a black dot
on a white curtain.

Slow Roasted

Love is too abstract for me,
like a chunk of modern art
or the clunk of sudden hearts

It should be slow-roasted
like a potato in an oven
or hard-boiled
like a matter of fact

God is too obscure for me,
like a crazy naked man
or the crack of aging hands

It should be re-paved
like a driveway in despair
or re-surfaced
like molecules of truth

Poetry is too banal for me,
like a wrist of a million wrinkles
or the cuff of a billion crinkles

It should be written again
like an unfolding promise
or laid out before us
like a table-topped with hope.

Lumps in Throat

Can be surgically removed
by cutting out
the frost, want
and travesty of
modern urban existence

There's Gold in Them There Poems!

Fools.

Barking By Neon

In a little town
north of Seoul in South Korea
there's a little place
called 'Booby-Booby Land'

Every Thursday night
you can see wives
walking their muzzled husbands
on leashes,
trying to stifle their howls

This Little Buddha

This little Buddha went to market.

This little Buddha stayed at home.

This little Buddha had prozac.

This little Buddha had none.

This little Buddha went to jail.

This little Buddha came home.

This little Buddha went to therapy.

This little Buddha stayed in bed.

This little Buddha went to Temple…

…and this little Buddha went wee, wee, wee all the way home.

Okay

To achieve this state
is the only kind of
enlightenment we can
be sure of.

Paint your walls white.
Put up nice art.
Pick out people who play guitars.
Choose a partner who likes trees (and/or brown bread).
Pay attention to the news.
Look out for low flying politicians.
Look out for the bombs in their eyes.
Beware the dripping mouths of prophets.
Beware poets of all sizes.

Follow these nine steps to salvation
and you will be

okay.

Rather be read.

rather be read
than red

rather be blue in face
than yellow with terror

rather be gray with gravy
than green with envy

rather be white with ghost
than blank with boredom

rather be read
than red.

<Plant a tree here>

This Should be Your Book of Poetry

Found a finger on the way
to work today.
Won't tell you
what finger;
won't tell you
whose finger –
a broken finger
in mid-point.

And the finger told me

You don't have a passport
You don't have a mirror
You don't have a fierce look
You don't have a brave face
You don't have a strong jaw
You don't have a cigarette
You ain't got a hope in hell

I put the finger
in my pocket
and skipped on up
the High Street.
I quit my job and
bought a television,
some new clothes, a pack
of fags, a haircut and razor.

And then the finger told me

You don't have enough Black friends
You don't have enough Jewish friends
You don't have enough Portuguese friends
You don't have enough female friends
You don't have enough disabled friends
You don't have enough gay friends
You ain't got a hope in hell

I followed the finger to a
a party, a disco,
a nightclub, a pub,
a chatroom, a message board,
a coffee house,
a market square,

a college, a ghetto
and a dating agency.

And then the finger said

You ain't got a sex life
You ain't got a pet
You ain't got an artform
You ain't got a vet
You ain't got a laptop
You ain't got the Net
You ain't got a culture
You ain't got a hope in hell

I took myself to a sauna,
a bath house, an alleyway, a
car park. I bought a brown lab,
an orange tabby, a blue snake
and a red rat. Bought a P.C.
a scanner, a printer, a Mac
Took myself to a gallery,
a library, a museum and back.

And then the finger pointed to a mannequin in a shop window.
And one of its fingers was missing.
And I said

You ain't got a body
You ain't got a bone
You ain't got a heart
You ain't got a home
You ain't got a Jesus
You ain't got a joint
You ain't got a purpose
You ain't got a point
You ain't got a hope in hell

And in you

For Every Jar of Mustard

We were shaking
in the drop of night.

You offered warm breath
and the comfort of a cigarette
to blast through the darkness.

And in you,
I saw the man I was becoming.

We were laughing
in the face of belligerence.

You offered hot thought
and the smoke of a joke
to cheat through to truth.

And in you,
I saw the man I was becoming.

We were retching
in the trauma of loss.

You offered careful words
and the promise of sanity
to tunnel through to safety.

And in you,
I saw the woman I was craving.

We were broken
from the moment we were born.

You offered a life
a path, a perspective and a poem
to get through it all.

And in you,
I saw the woman I was in love with.

We were standing
in the genius of repair.

You offered a chair
a pillow, a pint and a warm meal
to fill in the empty spaces.

And in you,
I saw the person I could never be.

Drowning in Your Own Saliva

It’s the truth.

You may as
well
swallow it.

Haiku 5

Eager in the rain
Eternity dropping hints
on every inch worm

Sobriety

For John

Into your blue mist I go.
Into your quiet eyes I flee.
Into your piercing comfort I rest.
Into your day dreaming of drink I think.

The Joy of Text*

It can be as
simple as four words
that come to you
in beeps:

Let's.

Make.

Love.

Tonight.

It can be as
simple as two words
that go
bumping back:

Yes.

Please.

* and she texted me 4 mins after I wrote this thing

Fall

Leaves only
fall when you
are watching.

They pick their
moment perfectly,

and commit the
ultimate sin

before your
very eyes.

The Tomato Speaks Out

...and if you call me

a 'fruit' one more time

I'm going to scream all over

your salad.

It's a Dog's Life

I don't believe in
re-incarnation but I do
accept that I might have to face
the harsh consequences
of that belief in my
next life.

Guddha's Secretary

Starring: Poor Wretched Poet as "**P.W.P.**"

Guddha's Secretary as "**G.S.**"

P.W.P. : *Well, can I see him?*

G.S. : *He's in a meeting at the moment.*

P.W.P. : *But he called me here.*

G. S. : *Well, I'm sorry but he's a very busy man – please take a seat.*

P.W.P. : *Is it because I painted the gates to heaven black instead of white?*

G.S. : *No, I think he thought that was funny, reminded him of his favourite band.*

P.W.P. *Do you mean the London Gospel?*

G.S. : *No, I mean the Rolling Stones.*

P.W.P. *Oh.*

- Intercom buzzes -

G.S. : *He's ready to see you now, Mr. P*

For Whom the Bell Tolle's

For Eckhart

If you hear a long droan…
…then that is the ego waking
And if you hear a slow ring…
…then that is the ego having breakfast
And if you hear a flat pong…
…then that is the ego burping
And if you hear a dull thud…
…then that is the ego farting
And if you hear a sharp ping…
…then that is the ego laughing
And if you hear a wet ting…
…then that is the ego wailing
And if you hear a muffled bong…
…then that is the ego sighing
And if you hear a drawn out drong…
…then that is the ego yawning

And if you hear nothing…
…then that is the ego sleeping

Triple Lunch Special

I told myself
I was
gonna
quit poetry
today and start
longer sentences.
Then, something happened, and, on the way home I discovered…
Apollinaire in my sandwich.
I picked out all these Russian
poets shouting up at me
and some French ones
laughing.

Imagine what it's like
to be
that bit of Brie
between the bread
and the butter:
squashed against the pickle,
holding the pages in place.
Imagine being
picked apart
like a
collection of
crumbs pressed
together to form an anthology.

I imagine it's like having a poem stuck
in the corner of your mouth.

All the arguments
between
the bacon
and the lettuce,
the tuna
and the mayonnaise,
the prawns and the poets -
all fighting hard to be heard!

Hearing nothing but
gnashing teeth
from the people
who swallow you whole,
nothing but choking throats
spitting out the parts they don't like.

Apple Core

I

heard they

took a

bite

out of

each side…

Such Sun

Such sun as I have
seen.

Such sun.
Such sun.

Such sun as I have
seen.

Such sun.
Such sun.

Such is the sun
that I have seen.

Not Aborted

My ma' & pa'
sat me down
last night.
Da' looked up
at the sky and Ma'
took hold of my
hand.
Son, they said,
we got something to say.
After a pause
they continued:
Son, you were not aborted.

And you know
with these five short words
they explained
the last thirty years
of my life.

Marked for Life

I've always been a bit of a
Beatlebum.
I think about John Lennon a lot.
But I'm not the only one.
I can't really decide
if I love or loathe him.

It pains me to admit
what a horror he could be:
the way he treated Cynthia,
Julian, Sean…
The near and the dear ones.

If you look at pictures of him
towards the end of his life
you'll notice four things:

- a collapsed nasal passage
- a striking resemblance to Yoko
- a stack of old bones.
- he looks marked for death

The sad truth is that
the cocaine collapsed
his nasal passage;

He was emotionally dependent on
Yoko and as we are told
couples who are dependent on one
another start to look the same.

His appetite was
diminished to crackers
because of the drugs.

Mark Chapman took a man
away from us who was
afraid of the sun.

This is all very depressing.
This is all very wrong.

The good news is thus:
in his very last interview
he said he wanted to
live forever.

He asked for some
chicken soup, again
and again and again.

Always remember the slightly fatter
John with the cheeky grin.

Always look at early pictures
of John…

Never a Dull Roman

Keep your spirit still –

Though it bursts about
        in laughter
Though it trains around
        disaster

Keep your spirit still –

Though it hops about
        in heartache
Though it drowns around
        in black lakes

Keep your spirit still –

Though it balks about
        in bullshit
Though it stalks around
        in dulcet tones of yellow terror
        in broken bones of purple weather

Keep your spirit still –

Though it marches
        on without you
Though it panes the glass
        within you

Keep your spirit still –

Though it chars the path
        behind you
Though it mars the way
        before you

Keep your spirit still –

Though it zips you
        up in cliché
Though it nestles you
        in niches

Keep your spirit still –

Though it buggers you
    to boredom
Though it tempts you
    into whoredom

Keep your spirit still –

Though it lashes you
    to pieces
Though it hibernates
    in faces you have seen before
    in places you have licked the floor
    in questions you have silenced or,
    in Romans you have - till now - ignored

Keep your spirit still –

    in the sex of laughter
    in the cattle of courage
    in the eunuch of each thought
    in the prostitute of poetry
    in the bling of serotonin
    in the cancer of impatience
    in the murder of silence
    in the pulse of each word
    in the drip of each dot
    in the soot of every spirit

Keep your spirit still –

and you will be
    in every moment,

and you will be
    in every moment

Never a Dull Roman.

Rubber

all the world's an elastic band :

flick it to me.

Talk is Cheep

Too many writers
Talk

When they should be
Writing.

I know.
I'm one of them.

I can't afford to
do it anymore.

The Man in The Mirror

Wherever I go,
E'go,

Wherever E'go
I go.

III

Duel: Citizen

Oh to be a quiet man.

Punching Bag

I talked to Jackie.
She is punching bag.

I talked to Greg.
He's been up all night.
He is punching bag.

I talked to Stammers.
He told me as much.
Be bold! Punch it!
He is punching bag.

Took the D.L.R. to see Peter in Greenwich.
Everyday the same. Everyday the Anvil.
Punching Bag. Punching Bag.

Called Chris at the P.B.S.
How are you Chris?
I'm well, moving to Japan:
Have punched the bag in London.
Will be punching bag in Asia!

Had a beer with Booth.
10 years in Russia.
5 punching keyboards.
5 punching bags.

My dad,
never afraid of a letter.
Pun. Chin. Bag.
Punch in bag.
Punching Bag.

My mother,
the other poet in the family.
She, of course,
punching bag.

Then the rest of the gang came bruising up the street.
All of 'em ready for a fight:

Rebecca pulling staples out of couches.
Punching Bag.

Mark in his truck with no steering.
Punching Bag.

Maddy with the Thames in her pocket.
Punching Bag.

Rob chewing on his salt farm.
Punching Bag.

Coyote on Augusta.
Punching Bag.

Goodyear lining up his lens.
Punching Bag.

Connolly digging the truth out of monsters.
Punching Bag.

Toronto in its tilting.
Punching Bag.

Stu dipping a lady in Buenos Aires.
Punching Bag. Punching Bag.

England peeling back its eyelids.
Punching Bag.

Canada kicking raccoons off its doorstep.

Punch. In. Bag.
Pun. Chin. Bag.
Punching Bag.

Safe Art

The y make safe art,
com fort able art,
armchair art
for armchair pee-pole.

" A long necklace
to go with
a short cardigan."

Birth of a Crap Poem

Created at 10:01 am 30/03/07
Cremated at 10:02am 30/03/07

Death of the Author

I read about this theory.
Wrote about it.
Told all my friends
and family about it.
Told them to forget about
me,
to focus on the novel.
I sent out letters,
waiting for no response.
Mum wrote back in Caps
Lock:

DAD THINKS YOU'RE
A LUNATIC!

Hard Water

Whether it be the
calcium build up
around the shower head
in Toronto
or the lime-scale
excuse for the
bottom of
the kettle in Sheffield,
we can be sure that
the inside of our
stomachs
are lined with the
same chalky mess

wherever we bathe
wherever we drink
wherever we shave
wherever we think

The Marmite Trap

what happened? oh shit

seemed like only
yesterday
we were drinking out
of high heels,
lacing up the leathers
for another
crack-o-the-whip,
pinning up posters
to advertise the monsters.

19 Nervous Breakdowns later...

now we're cleaning
out marmite pots,
so clean we can
look right through
them - turning them
into jars for paper clips,
rubbers, broken pencils.

19 Nervous Breakdown later...

now we're making fun
of Londoners –
can't even joke about
bombin' the place no more.
Now we're becoming
like Vincent in his
disgust for Paris.

oh shit

even our walls are yellow.

Sound of Beards Cracking 1

Two hours of television
takes two days of meditation
to remove.

About the same time it
takes to grow a full beard.

Tired.
          Fat.
Roman nose.
          Ugly.
Black Teeth.
          Sleeping-bag eyes.

Two days of self-reflection
and no beard to
show for it.

She as a Warm, Soft Night

She as a warm, soft night

Who am I to
hang out moons to dry?

She as a thick, black puddle

Who am I to
stir up a nightmare?

She as a tin can rolling up to curb

Who am I to
walk among the rubbish?

She as a soft, little irony

And who are we to
take a stab at the clouds?

She as a stomach gone empty

And who am I to
grumble?

She as a nothing blade, made of nothing smoke & nothing mirrors

And who am I to
doubt her?

She as the queen of the hips & lips & legs & breasts

And who are we to
put a face on creation?

Profita Margins

German Hans had these eleven
profita rolls (*yum, yum*)
He wanted four
but only ate three
and took the rest into work.
German Hans asked them to leave him one.
Susan ate three.
Daryl ate four.
Wendy ate one.
Altogether, they ate eight.
German Hans had only one word
to describe his sense of loss....

...NINE!

Love

Ignore it.

If it's still there
by morning
see a Doctor
or a Lawyer.

Or both.

Megalomaniac

Usually on Sundays,
On a park Bench,
Beneath the old Oak Tree
that every English village has.

When no one
is looking.

Easter Ugly

I see it.
I see it for
all it is.

My shriveled
fingers.
My raccoon
eyes.

She sees it.
She sees it for
all it is.

Her freckled
neck.
Her diamond
tits.

He sees it.
He sees it for
all it is.

His wretched
mouth.
His pink-faced
wit.

We see it.
We see the
point where ugliness
starts to make sense.

My vacuous gob.
Her decedent ass.
His relentless cheek.

Class 4B

The best day of my life
was when I realised I was no
more important than Spencer
the spastic kid at number 29.

(This is the part where
you get a lecture on 'Political Correction')

That was the day I realised
that I really had legs,
I really had arms,
I really had a mouth
that didn't dribble.

(This is the part where Trevor
sniggers at the back of the class)

Until that time,
I thought Spencer
was unlucky but well looked after.
Then I realised that Spencer
was just well looked after.

(This is the part where
the sniggering stops).

You see Spencer was
the brother of one of my classmates
the son of two human beings,
a creature that was being kept
alive by a breathing apparatus.

(This is the part where 'luck'
has nothing to do with being)

Piece of Ass VS. Peace of Mind

Fellas.

you will come up against this
you will ask yourself hard questions
about the flesh and the fulfillment
it offers you
you will be 24, 25, 26
and say, *'the sex never ends -*
it's like an untapped river'

and then another part of you speaks,
it says, *'i think i know*
what this is about;
i think it's about time
i addressed this'

then you will make
several more mistakes,
you may be 34, 35, 36
until you can correct them.
the river dries up
and you spit out sand

Fellas.

Then you know.
Then you can be certain.
Then you can retrace your
steps back to the well
and look into your reflection.

Or into the eyes of your first-born.

Sound of Beards Cracking 2

Lived a life of
silence and probability.
Had a tense time of it.

Rubbed face a lot.
Scratched skull
to bits.
Flakes came off in
hand.

And when it all
got too much.

When you worked
out the where each
noise came from.

Sat there in silence…..

……listening…..

….to the sound…..

…of
        your
                beard
                        coming
                                through.

Words are for Windows

As a petulant writer,
words are everything.

As a bus-stop Buddhist,
words are useless.

As a desperate human,
they're all I've got.

Words are for Windows 2

As a tiny Englishman
words are my heritage,
As a cranky Canadian
they come in two sizes: English & French,
As a citizen of the world,
words get in the way of road signs.

Truth

We go to bed each night.
We wake up each morning.
We know too many things
already.

Ko Samui – *Thailand (May, Oh Six)*

Looking out through yellow curtains.
Looking out on Buddha's Beach.

Got no clock,
no compass,
no clue what colour
the sand is.
Just Gauguin's yellow curtains.
Just a line of endless planes
in a holding pattern.

Get drunk. Sleep hard.

Between the waves and the
thunder and the 747's
my dreams stretch out
like seven minute Fellini's.
Have to burp myself
each morning.

Sleeping Brother
Sleeping Brother…

James is persistent.
James rearranges the room,
cranks up the air-con,
lines up the sunglasses,
sorts out the boys' beer
from the mens' milk,
slaps his Buddha's belly
and falls back asleep.

Breakfast time.
The waitress.

Look at the smiling
creature before me.
Look at her for something green.
She hands me a white menu
and a silver fork
and wishes me good morning.
So many planes I say
and it's a laugh in return

not a ‘yes’ or a ‘no’
or a *so many planes* back.

We like Eggs.
We like them with the shell crushed in.

The menu represents
my life options:
a mango royal is a
career in advertising;
a croque monsieur
a wife in Woking;
a Bangkok Burger
an early death;
an Omlette
some crushing truth.

It’s too early
to eat.

Another plane goes over
my head
- *every seven minutes* -
another plane,
another plan.

A Certain Special Someone

A friend from Toronto
came to see me in England.

She could see I was thinner.

A friend came across
the Atlantic for dinner.

I could see she
was whiter, warmer, a writer:
a winner.

A friend came to
England, so happy,
a grinner.

She could see I was
a ghost of my former self:
a sinner.

A friend came to
dinner this winter,
for Pinter and wine
and dinner at mine

I could see she
was less of a mess than before
brighter, bolder, older, golder:
a born-again beginner

A friend came for Pinter
and winter and wine and
dinner was *in-her*
but frozen in time

<You see it was love
but I couldn't win her>

The Middle Way

Middle-class
Middle-english
Mid-atlantic
Mid-poem

Amid all of this
we remain

(we admit)

middle of the road.

Cough-free Carnivore Vs. Vegetarian Smoker

Eve smells
giblets on
Adam's breath

Adam can't
get past the chimney
in Eve's hair

Most of the Poets

Mostathepoetsiknow
are red in the face
from standing under streetlamps

Mostathepoetsiknow
are grinning like chocolate
for a place in the glovebox

Mostathepoetsiknow
are pleading with tigers
after a night on the town

Mostathepoetsiknow
are cranky mutherfuckers
who don't eat enough protein

Mostathepoetsiknow
are living off silence
and dancing in the gaps

Mostathepoetsiknow
showed up three lifetimes ago
and got caned on corked wine

Mostathepoetsiknow
have tabs in every pub, whorehouse,
boozecan, speakeasy, abortion clinic, jail

Mostathepoetsiknow
would give up their Christian names

for a bowl of identity

Mostathepoetsiknow
shuck their souls like clams
into dangerous waters

Mostathepoetsiknow
have their eyes clamped,
their teeth, their brains and their cars

Mostathepoetsiknow
exchange bits of broken metal
for a notepad and an erection

Mostathepoetsiknow
grow up, have babies, wives,
kitchen sinks, kitchen sunks

Mostathepoetsiknow
dread rivers and puddles
for the wriggly things in them

Mostathepoetsiknow
kick back at the television
and swear at the newspapers

Mostathepoetsiknow
get government bacon
from government pigs

Mostathepoetsiknow

are unpublished hacks,
with drug habits and bad hair

Mostathepoetsiknow
turn away from humanity
in a fit of despair

<Deep Breath In>

Most of the poets I know
are terribly nice chaps
with terribly nice caps

Most of the poets I know
are wrinkled and old
and covered in gold

Most of the poets I know
are good for a moment
then begin to ferment

Most of the poets I know
have published their works
and taken office jobs

Most of the poets I know
kneel down before a woman,
a child, a dog, a church, a god

Most of the poets I know
are terribly nice people

with views of the steeple

Most of the poets I know
want the world in nice roses
and the words in nice rows's

Most of the poets I know
have bitten the dust
are starting to rust

Most of the poets I know
are greg, aidee, nigel, tom,
elisabetta, jackie, valerie, dom

Most of the poets I know
are happy with life
but fed up with the public

Most of the poets I know
are *"romantics, nancies,*
depressives, queers

dreamers, idlers, pussies,
pansies, charmed, disarmed,
hapless, benevolent, middle-class, piers'

Mostathepoetsiknow
are white in the face
from being out of the spotlight

<Deep Breath Out>

Pouring Curry Onto a Swan

That swan didn't come round today.

The river separates the council houses
from the canal boats.

I'm throwing my seed into the water at ducks
watching people divide up their picnics.

How nice to take a baguette down the river.
How nice to climb inside that baguette.
with the lettuce and the tomato and the pubic hair.
How nice to row a baguette down the river with your loved one.

What a good-looking day you are.

From the estate we have a wonderful view.
We scribble our views underneath the bridge…

We throw rocks at passers-by and
smash florescent lights onto the gravel path.

I watch joggers go crunching by.
In that crunch I hear myself.
In that satisfying crunch I have a voice.
No wonder that swan don't come round no more.

Last week I threw a vat of hot curry onto it.

The Crunch of Karma

You go to great pains
to jump over
brother snail

only to land
on sister

Sustaining Canada

Think big
but let go
of the ghost
once it reaches
America

Jam @ Clapham Junction

Jam in hair
Jam on hands
Jam under nails
Jam under eyelids

The Music of a Weightless Pedestrian

The poet is not a 'little god.'... He is not picked out by a mystical destiny. ... The best poet is he who prepares our daily bread; the nearest baker who does not imagine himself to be a god. Pablo Neruda

Bring me the Human Heart
Bring me a traffic jam
Bring me a haircut, a nice one from the eighties
Bring me a moustache, a beard, both
Bring me a mirror
Bring me Intellectual Unrest
Bring me the dumbing down of my people
Bring me the words, *avalanche, dogmatic, impulsive*
Bring me a Headline from every National Paper
Bring me a Love Letter, a Gas Bill, a Bank Statement
Bring me all the Junk Mail in America
Bring me a furnace, a shredder, a landfill
Bring me the colour yellow
Now bring me the colour blue
(You see what you have)
Bring me red wine and black Guinness
Bring me a shamrock
Bring me a blade of grass
Bring me a grain of sand
Bring me a pepperoni pizza, a nice one from the nineties
Bring me an Englishman, an Irishman, a Scot
Bring me a joke
Bring me mercy
Bring me a Dutch toilet with two flushes
Bring me a coffee and a doughnut
Bring me a Canadian accent with cheese on top
Bring me a Chihuahua
Bring me an elastic band
Bring me a bicycle, a circus, a Russian Bear
Bring me Guildford on a Tuesday at two thirty-five
Bring me Happy Hour
Bring me Queen & Spadina at three in the morning
Bring me streetcars every six minutes
Bring me Adolph Hitler, Mugabe, Bush, Blair
Bring me Formica tables
Bring me the Human Rash
Bring me the tongue of a poet
Bring me the black dot at the end of a sentence.

So She Broke into a Run

The wallet went missing.
Kept it on a chain.
The girlfriend went missing.
Kept her at arms length.
So we all joined hands
and formed a search party.
Found the wallet
but not the girlfriend.

Kept a picture of her on a chain.
But she wanted to be free.

So she broke into a run...

Haiku 6

England will come
dripping to us when we go
dripping to her

Old Age

Your face looks like a collapsed wedding cake.
Your knitting looks like an old scrotum.
The best reaction to our nails
growing longer
is sheltering
silence
and
warm
acceptance.

Frequently Asked Questions
(4th Anniversary of invading Iraq)

March 20, Oh Seven

They F.A.Q.'d Iraq
With their usual cack
Of if in fact
The Weapons of Whack
Are still in tact

So FAQ Iraq
with all the Kings Horses
and all the Kings Quacks
and all the Armed Forces
and all the Big Macs

They F.A.Q.'d Iraq
Spin Doctors & Hacks
By crying out wolf
So George can play golf
And launch an attack

So FAQ Iraq
don't cut em no slack
because our little leaders,
our nasty vote needers,
are lacing the track
with the best kind of crack.

They F.A.Q.'d Iraq
By painting it black
Like Oil, in fact
I bet they won't get
A better shellac

So FAQ Iraq
with all the Kings Horses
and all the Kings Quacks
and all the Armed Forces
and all the Big Macs

<Pop go their heads
Snap go their backs>

To My Explosive Pal Greg

My pal.
Buddery.
My word.
You – *wandering about Verona* –
lost to time and space,
making plans for
the mafia in your
mind.

How many milligrams must I tell you?
How many milligrams must you tell me?

I hope you're safe.
I hope you're safe.
I hope we can
spit at each other's verse.
I hope you can wander
your way back to Wordsworth
and stay on planet earth.

We're looking at the same suns exploding.

How many milligrams of Mustard do we need?
How many milligrams of Mustard do we
have to measure out?

We're looking at the same moons in motion.

How many milligrams of hope must it take?

We're measuring out the same distance to the salt
in our heads.

Last Pebble for England *(Nov 9, Oh Five)*

Back to hard water,
To the land of sandwiches.
Yes, you grew out of it.
Back to the polished tracks
Of South West trains.
Back to the farmer's market
On cobbled streets
That stick up like horses hooves
Buried upside down.
Back to the roads
Put down by people rubbing
Cement into their eyes.
Back to the flaring nostrils
Of the long-jackets on the High St,
To the glaring pint glasses
Of the working-class Kings.

They are no longer in robes.
Nor jackets. Nor trains. Nor nostrils. Nor sandwiches.

There's a pretty girl on the train.
She's taller than me.
She grew out of coloured hair.
She grew out of studded bracelets.
She grew out of spikes in lip.
She done with all that.
She's going to Worplesdon.
She's done with all that.
Yes, she grew out of it.

Back to the radiators,
To the robes that we hang over them,
To the corners of the room where it's warm.
Back to the hard water,
The lime-scale build-up covering everything in sight:
Sinks, mugs, kettles, toothbrushes, teeth, tongues.
Back to the fixed stares of the jackets on the platform
(where the concrete has set in their eyes)

Back to the radiators
That we backed ourselves up against,
Burning our fingers, chipping off paint,
Where the rust has come to us
Like a baby giving birth.

You grew out of her.
She grew out of you.
That baby grew up,
Became somebody
And gave birth to another baby
And named it
And told it to live
And taught it to shop
And told it to stand in the corner.

You grew out of nostrils that were too big,
Out of ears that refused to listen.
You grew out of eyes that were full of concrete:
Full of soot and tar and fog.
You grew out of baggy sweaters
Into tight fitting jeans.
You grew out of it all.

It won't let you think anymore,
It will stop right there
And say, *Darling,*
This is self-indulgent:
I thought you grew out of that!

Back to *hi-ya's*
And watches that you
Flick with your finger,
Watches that you shake
With your fist to keep ticking.

Ah Tired

These poems are tired,
Ah tired.
These words are yawning,
Ah, so tired.
This poet tired,
Ah, such heavy eyes.
These words are sinking,
Ah, so very sunk.

Thirty-Five

I know that red bag of blood
will burst.
I know that my chest will cave in;
that my lungs will collapse
with the weight of the want,
because that blue bag of O,
that purple vein of A,
has a mind all of its own
and nothing I can do will stop it.

Your body arcs out towards the
blood red sun;
your body stretches away from
the rest of its breath,
because it has a mind all of its own.
Nothing I can say will stop it
from leaning.
Your body asks me no favours.
Asks nothing of me.

One of two things will happen
when I am thirty-five:
either I will come to
some volcanic realisation,
some definitive okey-dokey,
some small nod of certainty
and I will smile.

Or,
that lunging bag of blood and muscle
will burst inside my chest
and cave in my nipples
and tear away from the rest of my body.
It will come to a thumping halt.
It will finish.
It will stop.
It will compare itself
to an O type planet,
to an A type molecule
and puncture itself
for the hellovit.

Nothing I can do will stop it from
stopping.

Thirty-five is my locker number.
It always has been.
It has always pushed its way into my day
so that, when I look at a clock
and it says 9:35, I know it is a
good time to think:
'it's a good time to think'

So I think.

There are five sevens in my phone number;
I buy all these irreverant t-shirts
and shorts and the bill comes to thirty-five.
This always happens to me.
In Toronto, I filled my van
with $35 dollars of petrol
and cursed the meter
when I went a penny over.
I put all my worldy faith
into this number.

I wake up 7:35, 8:35, 9:35, 10:35…..

I know when I am thirty-five
that I will have something given to me,
have something taken away;
that I'll forget about my locker number.
That, after thirty-five situps,
that red bag of hope and sorrow will conk out.
It will look like a heart attack
or a blocked bit of nonsense
but when it becomes clear
that I died at nine thirty-five
then they will know.
They will know that there
was nothing to stop
that blue ball of blood
from rolling away
like a marble down a drain.

Behind every sandwich is the question of the Maker.

This will happen with certainty.
It might not. I can never be sure.
Sorry. About the confusion.
If this does not happen
then I will change my locker number.

It’s a stubborn little universe;
an arsy bastard of wants and wishes,
of impossible prostitutes,
stretching themselves endlessly before you.

This is hilarious to me.
LOL.

Short History of the Group Hug

It

here.   starts

ends   here

and

Gareth Strachan grew up in England and Canada. He has worked as an actor and a farmer, as a teacher and a bookseller. More recently, he has collaborated with The Guildford Book Festival, organising events involving writers and poets from across the country. At present, he is under the service of Her Majesty the Queen…as a Royal Mail postman. This is his first book of poetry.

'Pedestrian Poetry' involves the general public reading out random works in front of a camera. Excerpts can be viewed at www.pedestrianpress.co.uk. If you would like to find out more about this project or comment on this collection, please email info@pedestrianpress.co.uk - all feedback welcome.

<Your thoughts here>